HOWLERS

Robin Williamson

drawings by
Raymond Mullan

THE
BLACKSTAFF
PRESS
BELFAST AND WOLFEBORO, NEW HAMPSHIRE

First published in November 1987 by
The Blackstaff Press Limited
3 Galway Park, Dundonald, Belfast BT16 0AN, Northern Ireland
and
27 South Main Street, Wolfeboro, New Hampshire 03894 USA
Reprinted November 1987

Printed by The Guernsey Press

British Library Cataloguing in Publication Data
   Holy howlers.
      1. Religious education — Anecdotes,
      facetiae, satire, etc.   2. Examinations —
      Anecdotes, facetiae, satire, etc.
      I. Williamson, Robin
      200'.76   BV1471.2

Library of Congress Cataloging-in-Publication Data
   Williamson, Robin, 1935–
      Holy howlers.
      Summary: An illustrated collection of humorous
   mistakes and misquotations taken from religious
   examination papers.
      1. Christian education — Northern Ireland — Anecdotes,
   facetiae, satire, etc. [1. Christian education —
   Wit and humor]   I. Mullan, Raymond, ill.   II. Title.
   BV1470.G7W55   1987   268'.0207   87-18377

ISBN 0-85640-388-1

FOREWORD

This book began the day I lost my temper. I was shouting at a youth whose exam paper I had just marked. The rest of the class sat in awed silence. The boy tried to speak but I wouldn't let him get a word in edgeways. I still have a sense of guilt about the incident.

The question asked was: 'Complete the following quotation – "It is easier for a camel. . ."' The answer should have been '. . . to pass through the eye of a needle than for a rich man to enter the Kingdom of Heaven'. That unforgettable boy had written '. . . to pass water than to sleep'. I thought he was being too smart for his own good.

However it was my fault. When I calmed down he explained. I had said that camels could travel for a long time without stopping to drink, so 'It *is* easier for a camel to pass water'; and I had told the class that the Arabs found camels useful as watchdogs around their camps at night, so 'than to sleep' seemed reasonable when it was explained.

The questions examiners ask are often at fault too. 'John the Baptist's father was called. . .?' Answer: 'Mr Baptist.' Ask a stupid question. . .

Questions sometimes produce the most startling of answers. Usually it is a fault in teaching technique, or a desperation response by the young person taking the exam, or even a unique form of expression. When they are asked 'Who did Mary visit before Jesus was born?' and they answer 'The angle who was to be Jesus's Daddy' they are not exactly wrong but they will get no marks.

Over about twenty years these eccentric answers have made all that marking rewarding. Wading through the same question thirty or forty times can be very boring but these gems have kept me at it. The young people will live in my memory as long as *I* live, and I pay tribute to them: not laughing at them, but with them, in their misinterpretation.

These 'quotations' have provided the basis for a lot of talks I have given to a wide variety of organisations; they have amused many a staffroom and meeting of teachers. I hope you find them amusing too, and in your enjoyment give thanks to a couple of generations of wonderful young people. The vast majority of our youth are marvellous and I thank God for the privilege of having taught them.

Robin J. Williamson, 1987

What verse is missing from the Gospel of Saint Luke
in the
Revised Standard Version?

I think it is verse 24 but it is probably the
Old Testament.

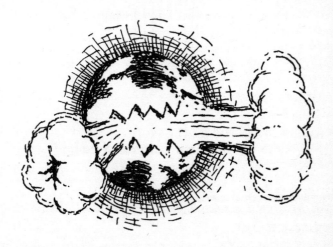

What God has joined together. . . must fall apart
someday, like his world.

1

The way man started out was as Adam and Eve in the garden of Eden without a care in the world but a fig leaf.

God so loved the world that. . . he left the women alone with Adam in the Garden of Eden.

What does Genesis Chapter One teach us about man and creation?
That we should pray to God to keep the population down to one each.

The men of Gibeon pretended that they had been on a long journey when they came to ask Joshua for his help. Joshua believed their lies and gave them new shoes, like trainers with no tops on them.

After many days the Ark stopped on top of a mountain. It was called Mount Anorak.

When they looked across the River Nile they saw that Moses was a little basket floating down the river while the soldiers were looking for him.

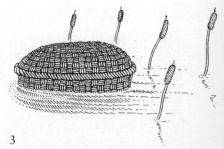

3

What did Jesus teach about evil thoughts?

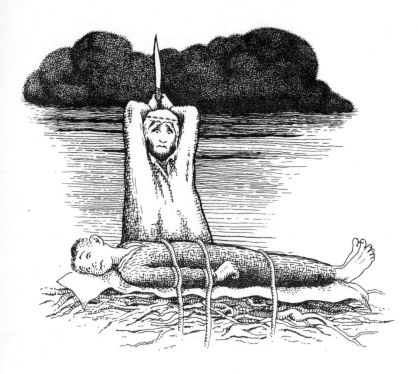

Isaac had evil thoughts when his father Abraham was going to kill him on the altar. He thought, 'God this is going to hurt me. I wish God would speak to my father and tell him not to stick the knife into me I am too young to be killed.'

How did Moses influence the Battle of Rephedim?
By getting married.

Choose one of the Commandments and explain what it means today.
You shouldn't take anything that belongs to your neighbour. This means that you shouldn't steal your neighbour's cow or the lawn mower or go in when he is not in and chat up his wife.

Write out in your own words the Commandment which is connected with greed.
If you have two coats give one of them away to please God and if you have two maidservants lend one of them to your brother and the same for wives too.

The story of the Burning Bush tells us that God is a very persuasive man. No matter how tired God was and no matter how Moses tried to get out of it God still said to him again and again, 'Stop grumbling Moses. You're going back to the land of Egypt for my people and arguing here with me will make no difference. You're going back. So go when you're told.'

Why did Moses remove his shoes at the Burning Bush?
God told him to take them off because he was standing on God's right hand at the time.

Why did Moses remove his shoes at the Burning Bush?
God told him he did not need them any more and his bare feet would do on the hot ground.

What instructions did Moses give for the Feast of the Passover?

He told them to trick the angle by putting something over the top of their door and emptying their drawers ready to flee when he gave them the word.

Describe the Passover Feast.

The angel of death would fly over the houses looking for the red cross sign which would tell him (her) (it) which houses to avoid in his search for child casualties.

Describe one incident in the history of Israel when they broke a Commandment?

The children of Israel made a Golden Calf while Moses was away up the mountain getting the Ten Commandments from God himself. This incident caused God to lose his head, but since Moses had not brought the Commandments to them from God they had never heard the one about making graven images. Certainly it was a terrible time for the children of Israel and God lost the bap so they must have broken his Commandment.

While Moses was in the mountain getting the Ten Commandments there came a mighty thunder and all the people waiting for him further down the mountain quacked.

Moses told the Children of Israel to get ready to flee when he gave the signal and to eat young lambs with sandals on their feet.

The Children of Israel were told by Moses to be ready to leave at a minuets notice.

The Children of Israel on their last night in Egypt put on their caps and scarves reddy to go fast when Moses sounded the hooter.

What did Manna look like?
White globs of sticky bread.

What did Manna look like?
It was found on the ground and looked like small round objects.

Moses was overworked in the desert trying to sort out the fights among his people. His brother told him he looked knackered.

One day Potiphar's wife pulled up her clothes and told her husband that Joseph had rapped her.

Potiphar had Joseph thrown into prison for causing adultery to his wife.

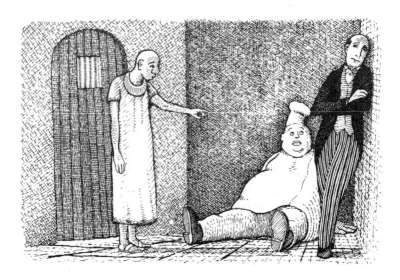

Joseph had been having an affair with Potiphar's wife without Potiphar knowing about it. But when he did find out he was far from pleased and put Joseph into prison with a baker and a dreaming butler.

Potiphar's wife took a real fancy to Joseph and made advances to him, but because he was a good man Joseph said no to the woman when she pulled at him, held him and kissed him. He escaped from her clutches but found that he was too tired to escape from Potiphar and his soldiers.

Joseph died when he was 110 years old and because of his great position in Egypt he was emballed and then placed in an Egyptian coffin which had a smaller box at the side for the missing pieces.

The Children of Israel were very fond of idolatry even though they knew more about the one true God than anyone else. Moses put three thousand men to death for the sin of idolatry. That was a thick crowd of sinners even for a great leader like Moses to get rid of but when Moses told them to stop worshipping idols they got thick with him and refused to obey so he said, 'Right that's it, me and God himself have had enough of this. Die!'

Why did the people say to Moses 'It would have been better for us to serve the Egyptians'?
Because the Egyptians paid their waiters better and they could earn more money.

How was King Ahab killed?
He was stabbed during a big battle with a steak.

Joshua led the Children of Israel as they marched around the city of Jericho. Every day for six days Joshua asked the tribes to join him in a round.

When the Walls of Jericho came tumbling down a new era began for the Children of Israel. Describe how their lives were to change.

The trumpets of the battle of Jericho sounded a new note for the Children of Israel. That note was a C sharp which pierced their ears and enabled them to hear the voice of God again.

15

Judge not. . . was a friend of Deborah when they judged the people of Israel.

In your own words tell the story of Jael and Sisera.
Sisera was a Canaanite General who was fighting Barak the General of the Children of Israel. Sisera was defeated by Barak and fled from the scene of the battle. He called at the house of Jael to ask for a drink. Jael gave him some milk and offered him the use of her bed because he was tired. Jael told him he was wrong to be fighting with the Children of Israel and to prove she was right she nailed his head to the floor with a tent peg.

Samson was a kind of Charles Atlas of his day with long hair and a Philistine woman.

Who killed King Saul?
A woman called Phillis Stein.

In order to get rid of Uriah, King David. . . slept with his wife.

Samson loved Delilah but she made all his hair come out and he became a baldy weakling.

Ruth lived with Naomi but at that time Boaz took a fancy to her. He watched her from behind the hedge. He went round the fields leaving her bits of straw to show he loved her with corn.

What was the 'sin' of Aachen at Jericho?
The sin of Aachen at Jericho was a dirty sin.

What did Aachen steal?
A clock, two bars of gold and a wallet.

Saul crossed Samuel's palm with silver to find out which way his ass had gone. Samuel told him not to worry his ass would be home ahead of him when he got back.

Why did Hannah place Samuel in the Temple with Eli?

He was put in the temple with Eli to give his mother peace and because Eli had been promised a wee boy by Hannah.

What was Saul looking for when he first met the prophet Samuel?

A job.

What was Samuel doing when Saul first went to see him?

Samuel was getting the dinner ready because there was to be a big feast that night and he didn't have a wife to peel his potatoes for him and to get the vegetables ready. He told Saul to set the table and stay for his dinner.

Describe in detail how Samuel and Saul first met.

Saul was travelling along a road when he got thirsty
and needed a drink. As time went by, travelling on the
road he got more and more thirsty. Then he met a man
called Samuel who told him that he was having a party
at his house and he could get a drink there. At the party
Saul got a drink when very suddenly Samuel told him
that he was full of God's Holy Spirit. Saul said he
wasn't but Samuel made him king anyway.

Describe in detail what happened as a result of David's popularity.

Everywhere he went David was troubled by his fans. He was treated like a pop star and the women would sing his hit tune 'Onward Christian Soldiers'. This made Saul very angry and even jealous.

How did King David capture the city of Jerusalem?
He surrounded it with lit torches in jamjars or vasses.

Nathan the Prophet told David to lay off Bathsheba. She was the wife of Uriah and not for his lovemaking. However David had already sent Uriah off to get himself killed in battle so that it would be alright to lovemake with Bathsheba as she wasn't being taken care of by her husband. David loved her very much and got a baby. The baby died. Nathan told them that it was their lovemaking that killed the baby so Nathan told him to lay off it for a while.

They didn't lovemake for ages but in the end had a very wise baby called Solomon who grew up to cut babies in half when he wanted to know the mother's name.

Nathan the Prophet told King David off for messing about with someone else's wife and he told him he should stick to his pet sheep.

The story that Nathan told was that the rich man could not bear to part with even one of his sheep. He stole one that belonged to his poor neighbour so that he could prepare a meal for his guest. From this story I understand that it is better to have sheep than neighbours.

Saul and David were having a contest with juveniles and everything was going smooth until Saul threw his juvenile at David's back and David knew that Saul was better with juveniles than he was so he ran away.

What job did Jereboam do under King Solomon?

He collected slaves from the tribe of Joseph.
Jereboam was very kind to the slaves he looked
after and often told them to stop work and have a
cup of tea and a piece.

Elijah was noted for his strong staff, bald head and
the way he flew through the air dropping mantels
over people.

On the top of a high mountain called Caramel was a lot
of balls who had come to attack Elijah. He told them to
get stuck in.

Ahab walked in the sins of Jereboam — what were those sins?

Worshipping idles, and making bulls of gold and loving Jezabel too much for his own good.

How was King Ahab killed?

He was killed in battle. Dogs came to Ahab's chariot and saw the blood from the arrow wound that had killed him. Then the dogs licked the bloody chariot as Elijah had said they would many years before. When his wife Jezabel called the dog over to her she saw its bloody tongue and thought, 'Oh God that's my husband's blood on that bloody dog's tongue.'

How did Jezebel die?

Jezebel died in bed with another man and Jehu's army were also there too.

Another great thing which Isaiah did was when he wrote a bit of music called handles Messiah in which the songs tell us that Jesus was expected to appear to lead the Children of Israel into battle against the Romans.

What did Jeremiah do to show the people what would happen to them at the hands of the Babylonians?

He bursted his pot jar until it leaked all over his feet.

Where did Solomon's wealth come from?

He collected coppers from the copper mines on the edge of the Arabian desert.

What advice was given to Solomon's son Reheboam?

Go easy on your people or they will give you a hammering. Your father Solomon kicked in the head of everyone that complained but they wouldn't let you do that to them so you had better give them some time off work at the building sites.

Naaman gave Elisha's servant leprosy to go with the presents he wanted for his master.

What did King Jehu do to Queen Jezebel?
He went to bed with her and then threw her out the window for the dogs to kill her.

One day Jeremiah was watching a man called a potter making potties from clay.

Why was Jeremiah called the weeping prophet?
Because he weeped his eyes out all the time.

Does a knowledge of the Bible serve any useful purpose in the modern world?

A detailed knowledge of the prophets of the Old Testament like Isaiah, Jeremiah or even Ahijah and Micaiah may be very interesting but you don't find many people interested in bringing it into everyday conversation do you? I have waited for two years for someone sitting by our fireside to bring up Jereboam or Ezra but it hasn't happened yet.

To whom did Luke address his Gospel?
The man who reads books
The Roman House
Centurion Street
Jerusalem

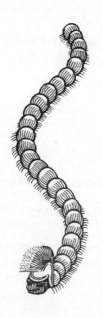

What is or was a Centurion?
A wee bug with a thousand legs.

What was the one thing the rich fool did not control?
His foolishness.

The angel Gabriel appeared to. . . come through the wall of the kitchen.

Zechariah was married to a good woman called Elizabeth. Unfortunately she was sterilised and was not as happy as she should have been.

Mary was getting aged and to have a child at her age was very nearly impossible, but God managed it.

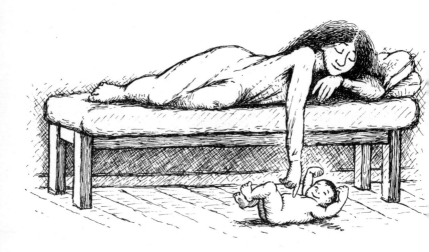

To begin with, Christ's birth was under his mother Mary who was a bit of a virgin.

The first angel appeared to tell Mary that she was pregurunt but Mary had already noticed.

What was the Annunciation?

The Annunciation was very unusual for the angle flew round the country to see Mary and Elizabeth and Joseph and Zack telling everyone of them that they were pregnant and could expect a very happy event in their families.

Then the angel Gabriel was sent by God to a virgin in Jerusalem (pop. 20,000) whose name was Mary.

Name the angel who appeared to Zechariah?
The angle what appeared to Zechariah was called
Garry and he came in a flash of light with some
good news.

Zechariah's wife was called. . . by the angel to get
pregnant.

When the angle told Zechariah that Elizabeth was going to have a son he was struck dumb because she was getting on in years.

What did the angel do to Zechariah?
Kissed him and whispered that he would be dumb and his wife would be pregnant as gifts from God himself.

Who did Mary visit before Jesus was born?

Her cousin Elizabeth because she had heard that
Elizabeth had fallen for a baby too and she wanted to
talk to her about it and her own position as an
unmarried mother.

*'My soul magnifies the Lord, and my spirit rejoices
in God my Saviour.' Who said this? Why was the
speaker rejoicing?*

These words were said by Elizabeth. She knew
about her cousin Mary having been visited and
made pregnant by an angel and she had some
baby clothes for her.

John inside Elizabeth's womb jumped up and
down when he saw Mary the mother of Jesus.
Elizabeth said, 'Hello, cousin Mary. How is the
Lord?'

*What was the message which the angel brought to
John the Baptist's father in the Temple?*

'Stay here in the temple for a while, I am going to
your house to get Elizabeth pregnant. . . Don't
speak or complain again until you get word from
me that I have done it.'

Zechariah was able to. . . see well ahead. . . after the baby was named John.

What name did the people want to give to Elizabeth's baby?

Fatherless infant of Mary's cousin.

What did the angels say to the shepherds the night Jesus was born?

'Hello shepherds. It's nice to see you. Could you point the way for people looking for a baby?'

$$\frac{Sin}{Cos} = Tan$$

What did the Heavenly Host sing when they announced the birth of Our Lord?

Songs.

Why did Joseph and Mary bring the baby Jesus to Jerusalem shortly after his birth?

To be censered and have its skin cut off by the priests in the Temple.

After his birth Christ grew up very quickly and at twelve years old he had the mind of a fifteen year old, which of course he used later in his life to perform miracles with.

How did our Lord live before he began his ministry?

Jesus Christ worked for his father i.e. Mary's husband in Nazareth. They were both carpainters and joyners but were really builders of houses and sheds and sheep dips.

What did Mary do when she found Jesus in Jerusalem talking to the doctors and lawyers in the Temple?

She cried for a while and then thumped him for disappearing like that.

What did Jesus do all night before he chose the disciples?
He walked around the place looking for them.

What did Jesus do on the mountain the night before he picked his disciples?
He wept and cried and prayed for some helpers with a bit of sense.

What happened when Jesus came out of the water after his baptism?
He was all wet.

Jesus said, *'No man can serve. . . good and bad food on the same plate.'*
He said this to show. . . that you cannot have a feast without washing your feet first.

Blessed are the peacemakers. . . they will make a lot of peaces.

Blessed be ye poor. . . but not as blessed as the people who are very rich.

Christians today are tempted to go to dances, booze-ups, gambling dives and the bingo, so that they can forget about temptations.

What did the shepherd do with the lost sheep?
He bandaged it up and set the dog on it to drive it home.

'No man can serve. . . bread alone.'

'Two hundred pennyworth of bread would not be enough to feed them.' When were these words said?

At the picnic the people were starving when Andrew said that two hundred pennyworth of bread wouldn't be enough. He forgot that Jesus had a trick up his sleeve which he did with five loaves and two fish.

Before the feeding of the five thousand Jesus was teaching a very thick crowd.

After teaching the crowds and feeding the five thousand, if it hadn't been for Andrew, Jesus would have missed the boat.

What did the guests think of the wine at the wedding feast in the town of Cana?
It was terrible wattery.

Jesus and his disciples were invited to a wedding in. . . order to see the presents and give their best wishes to the happy couple.

What did Jesus say great faith would do?

Great Faith would move anything that was in the way like hills and ships and anything that she thought needed to be moved.

What did Jesus mean when he said, 'This cup I give unto you'?
He meant, 'Here is a wedding present for you and your wife and thank you very much for inviting me to the wedding.'

Why did the girl think Peter was a Galilean?
When he spoke he was a bit thick.

Why did Levi give a party?
Everybody hated the sneaky wee Levi because he was a collector of taxes. Levi wanted to give them all some drink so that they would be nicer to him. When Jesus told the people that Levi was going to be one of his disciples they all laughed but Peter and John choked on their drinks and it went up Peter's nose.

John the Baptist deserved the words Jesus said about him: 'There is no greater forerunner than John that cometh from women forerunning.'

What miracle took place along with the gift of the Holy Spirit on the day of Pentecost?
It rained with thunder and lightning and the heavens opened up letting out a big bird which squacked into their ears with its hundreds of tongues.

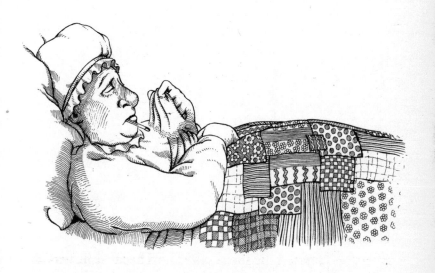

What do you know about Peter's mother-in-law?
She had a cold.

The temptation to jump from the Temple is the most important to Jesus. Satan just wanted him dead because Jesus was more powerful than Satan. He didn't tempt, He didn't jump and He didn't die.

Jesus was tempted again when the soldiers put him on the Cross and shouted, 'Right then, King of the Jews called Jesus of Nazareth, if you really are the Son of God get off that Cross and prove it.' Jesus didn't but He was.

The story about the tenants who threw their master's friends out of the vineyard is a very important story. My father has a house and his tenants won't give him his rent either.

Simon's partners in the fishing business were. . . greedy pigs and lazy chancers.

What happened on the boat that made the disciples afraid?
Jesus asked the disciples to walk on the water and they were afraid to try it. One of them – I think it was Simon Peter – tried it but when he followed him he fell in.

What was the ointment called with which the woman anointed Jesus?
The ointment which the woman used on Jesus was called greasy.

Whom did Jesus ask three times, 'Lovest thou me?'
He asked Mary when she was washing his feet
with very dear oil.

*What did Simon the Pharisee think when he saw the
woman washing the feet of Jesus?*
He thought, 'Jesus is alright there.'

What did Jesus say to the woman who anointed him?
'You are lovely and I liked it.'

Jesus said to the woman who anointed his feet,
'Your. . . loveliness. . . has saved you. Go in peace.'

Not long after arriving in the upper room for the Last
Supper party Jesus had his feet bathed in oil by a
woman, which seemed to happen to Jesus everywhere
he went in the Bible.

Death not only happens to everyone, it also
happens to living people as well.

What was the woman of Samaria doing when Jesus
met her?
She was sitting with Jesus at the well having a chat
about her adultery with a whole lot of men and how
she had adulterated them all to death.

What did Jesus do to help the poor widow of Nain?
He stopped the funeral that was passing and told the
dead man to get up and help his mother because she
was a widow woman. It was no time for her son to be
dead when she needed him.

What does the Gospel tell us that Jesus had to say about divorce?

The Pharisees came to Jesus about divorce and Jesus said that it was not a sin, it was just that man and woman cannot live in peace and happy marriage until they have divorce among them.

Write a paragraph on Jesus's teaching about marriage.

Jesus didn't get married. The girl he loved turned him down when her brother died because he took a long time to bring him back to life again. . . She still loved him and liked to rub his feet while he played with her hair.

When Jesus raised Jairus's daughter from the dead he. . . shouted at her, 'Get up little girl your dinner is ready.'

He brought his head on a charger. Whose head? What was a charger?

It was John's head. A charger is what the Americans call a till or a money machine.

Judas Iscariot was not really involved in the death of Jesus only he thought everybody should know where Jesus was and anyway Poncey Pilate would do him no harm anyway, so he wouldn't.

What were the names of the two sisters at Bethany that knew Jesus?

The two sisters were called Mary and Martha. They also had a brother called Lazy Russ.

The disciples at the transfiguration wanted to build three booths for Moses, Isaiah and Jesus. The booths were tents with boxing rings in the centre so that the audience could see the three contestants.

'I tell you, you are Peter and. . . you talk too much.*'*

Copy out one of the Lord's sayings from your memory.
It's all over and I am ready to drop into your hands Lord God.

What did Jesus say it was right to do on the Sabbath?
It was rite to go to Church and Sunday School but not rite to watch Television.

Jesus said, *'No man can serve. . .* the Lord without washing.'

What did Jesus do on the Sabbath day that angered the Scribes and Pharisees?
He went around helling people while their backs were turned.

Father forgive them. . . they are a terrible bad lot of sinners who do bad things to their mothers.

Jesus once. . . played some funny games with. . . children to show that he cared for all children.

Who said and when, 'Thou knowest that I love thee'?
When Jesus was waiting for his dinner he said it to Mary (or Martha) who had nothing to do except sit and talk to him while her sister (the other one) worked in the kitchen.

What is a hypocrite?

A hypocrite is the thing the doctor sticks into you. He sticks it into your arm, or into your bottom when you have an injection. Sometimes the nurse at school uses the hypocrite on me.

Jesus disliked the Pharisees and the Sadduccees because they were always hypocricising people.

Jesus understood Hebrew and he would have known some Latin and Greek but he actually spoke Aromatic.

It is easier for a camel. . . to walk than to run.

We have no King but. . . we have a Queen.

It is easier for a camel. . . to pass water than to sleep.

Tell the story of the rich man and Lazarus.
The rich man had an old carrot which God loved but
he ate it on his way to Heaven and God let him fall back
into Hell.

Name one outcast from society helped by Jesus.
Jesus helped ten leepers but only one came back to
thank him when Jesus made him a hole leeper.

Why did they 'marvel' at Him?

The people marvelled at Jesus because he cured the sick, raised the dead and had a mother who in her young days had been loved by God.

What miracle took place along with the gift of the Holy Spirit on the day of Pentecost?

Jesus performed a miracle by healing an old woman who couldn't straighten her back by shouting, 'Straighten woman! Straighten your back! Straighten up your sins are forgiven!' into her ear as he came up behind her.

Tell the story of the blind beggar.

This blind beggar came through the crowd shouting and swearing at Jesus, 'Come here you man of God give us the sight back. Let me see with one eye anyway.' He wanted to see so that he could go places and catch a bus again.

Jesus said, 'The sick need. . . to go to the hospital under the doctor.'

Explain: 'Thou art not far from the Kingdom of God.'
This means you don't look a bit well and you are going to die soon now.

It is easier for a. . . rich man. . . *to enter the Kingdom of Heaven than for a camel to go through. . .* the eye of a stone.

How many of the following quotations can you complete?

Not many. When I read them, none.

How did Jesus answer the young man who said, 'All these things have I observed from my youth.'

'My son, you have a lot to learn yet.'

The parable of the mustard seed tells us that mustard bushes can become really big and a lot of wee mustard pots can be filled there.

Jesus said it was harder for a. . . sinner. . . to enter the Kingdom of God than for a camel to go through. . . the eye of a donkey.

In the Parable of the Judge and the widow why did the Judge act on the widow's behalf?

The widow loved the Lord and this was the Lord moving in the Judge like a Holy fiery wind showing the Judge how to love the widow.

What did the woman who was a sinner bring to anoint Jesus?

A big ornament.

During his Ministry Jesus had no fixed abode but relied on his friends and other kind people to find him a squat.

Why was Martha annoyed when Jesus visited her house?

Martha was annoyed that day because she was doing the washing and didn't want any visitors to annoy her.

It is easier for a camel. . . to swim than for a fish to run.

It is easier for a camel. . . to live without water than it is for me.

'In my Name' – *what does this phrase mean?*
'In my name' means that in Roger McKee there is one 'O', one 'G', three 'E's, one 'M', one wee 'C', one 'K' and two 'R's.

Why did Jesus enter Jerusalem on a donkey?

Jesus entered Jerusalem on a donkey because the horse had been booked out already from the riding stable.

Write out and explain one Commandment which mentions 'your neighbour'.

Thou shalt not commit adultery against thy neighbour's wife when his back is turned.

Describe what you saw in the Episcopal church.

As we came round the corner from the door I saw a crook. The man in the long robes who was holding the crook by the shaft was a Bishop.

On the Cross of Jesus it was written, 'This is. . . the Jew who called Pilot names.'

Where two or three are gathered together in my name. . . This is called a Church, or a Temple, or a Sinagog, or a Gospel Hall.

Greater love hath no man than this. . . that I have for all men, and boys too.

Why were the disciples amazed when Jesus strode on ahead of them into Jerusalem?

The disciples were amazed because they had brung a dunky for him to ride into Jerusalem.

Repent and be. . . petrified.

What made Jesus angry when he visited the Temple the week before Easter?
The people who changed money in the Temple annoyed Jesus because of the way they robbed the people. Jesus wanted the money to be robbed by God.

Why is the Sunday before Easter called Palm Sunday?
Because the people cheered when Jesus came into Jerusalem. They clapped their hands by hitting the palms of their hands together when he walked on their old clothes.

Jesus wept over the city of. . . Bombay.

You cannot serve. . . him. . . *and. . .* me at the same time, son.

What did Jesus ask for to illustrate his answer to the question, 'Is it lawful to pay tribute to Caesar or not?'

He asked for a stick to thump the man with.

What was 'The Tent of Meeting'?

It was a tent put up on the edge of every village to have parties and good times in when the Children of Israel stopped to feed their flocks.

Why did Jesus condemn the man who had only one talent?

He condemned him because it was a bad talent.

Describe in your own words the value of belonging to a Christian Church.

The value of belonging to a Christian Church in the modern world is that it is easier to get christened, married and buried and you also have a chance to go to coffee bars.

Those whom God hath joined together... will never be broken apart because they are well stuck.

He who has seen me has seen. . . the new clothes my granny gave me for my birthday.

Whatever you wish that men would do to you. . . tell them what it is or they will never know what you want.

One of the first women to come to the tomb on the first Easter morning was. . . pregurent and scared to death.

Jesus pluffed his spit into the beggar's eyes and he immediately received his sight.

Why did Jesus say, 'Get thee behind me Satan,' to Peter at Caesarea Phillippi?

Jesus told Peter for Satan to get behind him at Caesarea Phillippi because he couldn't see what was going on.

What shall it profit a man if he gain the whole world. . . if he loses his life in a terrible accident.

What did Jesus say was necessary before the sick could be healed?

Jesus said that the sick need neglect.

What did Jesus teach about false prophets?

He taught that false prophets was no good because everything has to be paid for at some time and if there are no prophets there are no jobs.

How did Jesus sum up the Commandments?

Jesus summed up the Commandments when he said: 'There are ten Commandments and if you count them you will find that this is perfectly correct.' There is an eleventh Commandment but Jesus did not know it himself.

Why did Nicodemus go to Jesus by night?

Nicodemus had been busy all day. He was a lawyer and he didn't want to go until he could earn no more money from the people he was cheating during the day.

Give one reason why Judas Iscariot betrayed his master?

Judas betrayed his master because he needed the money and the hours he had to work were far too long anyway.

What did Jesus reply when Peter said, 'Lord I am ready to go with you to prison and to death.'

Jesus replied 'Don't bother yourself Peter I will be rising again on the third day anyway.'

What reminder did the two men give to the women when they came to the tomb?

A piece of paper with a short message on it from Jesus saying that he had gone on ahead into Heaven.

How did Judas indicate which was Jesus when he brought the soldiers and temple guards to Gethsemane?

He pointed with his finger. 'That's him there. That one crying his eyes out over by that olive tree.'

Before the cock crow twice. . . everybody is usually fast asleep.

What happened in the Garden of Gethsemane just before Jesus was arrested?
The disciples Peter, James and John fell asleep. When Jesus woke them up one of them said to Him, 'The day you gave is over so go to bed. We love you Jesus but we are knackered with all your teaching and praying and the party as well.'

What reminder did the two men give to the women when they came to the tomb where Jesus had been laid?

The two men who were wearing white suits told the women that they had just missed Jesus but not to worry too much that Jesus was not there, for he would be back to see them later.

Give one command which Jesus gave to his disciples?

There's a brave crowd of you so get out of here and start preaching the things I was telling you about God.

Who was present in the upper room at Pentecost?

Besides all the disciples in the upper room the landlady was also present. She must have been checking up on Jesus's friends at the party and she never saw Jesus arrive with the others.

What answer did the disciples give when they were asked, 'Why stand ye here looking up?'

Jesus and his angels will be flying past soon.

What were the last words of Jesus before he ascended to Heaven?

I'll be seeing you two later. Oh and John would you mind my mother until I come back?'

What reminder did the two men give to the women when they came to the tomb?

Jesus has left the tomb and ressurrected into Heaven without leaving a trace as you can see.

How did Mary Magdalene recognise Jesus in the Garden?

She recognised him because she knew what he was wearing and there was also a big hole in his hand when she shook it.

Who were the women at the tomb on the first Easter morning?

Mary the mother of Jesus Christ, Joannie and Mary MacDoolin.

In primitive countries food is often sold in unhygienic places but as we know in this country food should be covered when it is offered for sale because of the diseased types who buy it.

Describe the Passover Feast.

The first Passover was celebrated with Jesus sitting in the middle of the table with his disciples sitting on the floor round him.

Many young people forget about their grandparents and the fact that they may be lonely and may only send a card at Christmas. Little do they know that their grandparents may not have the strength to lift the card off the floor.

Joseph of Arimathea had a grave made for himself in readiness for when he should die himself, so he told Mary that he thought his grave would just do for Jesus and he would sell it cheap. Mary thanked him and it just fitted her son – God.

When he came out of prison his friends were shocked at Paul's emasculated appearance.

Pilate sent for. . . a bison and some soap. . . *to show. . .* the people that he could wash his hands for them.

What evidence is there of a belief in Christ today?

Today we see priests and churches everywhere and we go to Church. People from America travel over to preach the word of God to the people of Ireland. These preachers are called Morons.

No man who puts his hand to the plough and looks back. . . can keep the tractor straight.

How is a Christian supposed to treat an enemy?

To buy him a drink or his dinner after he has beaten him up and almost killed him.

Joining a group of Young Christians can be great fun. Few people who do not belong to such a group realise the fun you can have just messing around with others of the opposite sex who have the same ideas as you do yourself. A lot of young Christian people are brought together by just messing around. Young people who have met on these occasions have fallen in love and started families while helping others in the community.

Be ye wise as serpents and. . . funny as frogs.

My father does not believe in God. Every time the Minister calls at the door to visit us he turns down the television and hides behind the living room door. My mother says he hides because ministers bury people and he doesn't want to be buried.

What two proofs did Jesus give to his disciples that he was not a spirit?

He asked them to have a feel at his body.
He had a great sense of humour and made them all laugh by suddenly appearing in the room with them like a lit up spirit from a ghostly world.

Who was Caesar?

Caesar was my Uncle Frank's Alsation. It got poisoned by the neighbours for eating their grass.

When the Monks and Ministers get their order to serve God that is when the doubting starts. That is when they ask themselves, 'Will these pagans believe what I say?' That is when many Ministers and Monks know that the answer is No and they go and be farmers like Mr Loughridge.

What does 'Eloi, eloi, lama sabachthani' mean?
It means 'Hello, hello, my wee lamb, have you
come home for Sunday dinner?'. . . I think.

In India if an expectant mother will not go to the
ante-natal clinic provided by Christian Aid it is
better that she should go to her own doctor even if
he is really a witch doctor who after all is
responsible for her condition. Her own doctor even
if he is a bit coarse will know what to do for her for
he has done it many times before.

How could Morning Assembly be improved?

If I was Minister of Education I would ban Morning Assembly. I would also make it illegal for religion to be taught in any school. This would improve religion in the country because then you would find people sneaking into the toilets for a quick prayer instead of a smoke as they do now.

Give one example from your own life to show what it means to trust God.

I only pray to God at times of trouble in my life, like exams, even though it does not always work. The right answers in my exams come from God but the wrong ones come from the devil.